MW01644705

A note from the author

Thank you for picking up my book!
I am so glad to have you here. This is a great read for my survivors of abuse or sexual violence, and one that I think will be extremely helpful for your healing journey.

The first part is composed of poems, and following that, there are tips on healing from the severe trauma that we have had to endure, against our will. Additionally, I cover how to channel your pain into action, and how to fight for survivors rights, and bodily autonomy for all with a capacity for pregnancy.

As Roe v Wade was overturned at the end of June, it is necessary that we do NOT give up fighting for such an important cause.

Through going to rallies, hosting my own rally, and participating in the movement in many other ways, I am happy to shed some light on how you can heal through your activism.

WE WILL NOT GO BACK

WE WILL NOT BE SILENCED

-Tara Kaur Sachar

THE POETRY SECTION

------------------------.

TW:
sexual assault
addiction and other mental illnesses
suicidal ideation
self harm
dating violence

------------------------.

No one warned me

demons are everywhere
you never noticed before the age of 13
monsters under your bed
were never something to dread
because they didn't exist
at least, not in your head

you met the demons later on in life
but they weren't demons at first

they were exactly what you liked
they made you breakfast and were nice
sweet brown eyes filled with lies
so you stayed until
your throat grew tight
too closed up to speak
too closed up to breathe
waiting for some type of reprieve
waiting to receive
and learning you were deceived

it broke me
because I simply wanted to believe.

you were cunning
you were smart and to me, stunning.
we liked the same music
I was in a state of confusion
it appeared
that no one understood me like you.
I only now know this is not true.

demons come in the form of many shapes
sometimes it's a drug
sometimes it's laced
sometimes it's flashbacks
and sometimes it's nightmares
sometimes it's the boys who seem innocent with a
spontaneous flair
sometimes it's my brain
telling me to kill myself
sometimes it's other voices
who enter with stealth
it's the voice that tells you
to risk your health
it's the voice that you can never tell
to shut up.

you learned there were many more demons than you expected
and you have accepted it

but is this the movie I directed?
aren't I the director?
Where is my power?
you took it from me like a picked flower
we all know they die
when someone picks them out of the ground
stop picking me up.
you dragged me down.

demons come in pills and powders
demons come when you've been violated and feel
you've lost power
demons come when you drown out the pain
and they stay the same
while I'm simultaneously trying to change
no one warned me there were this many at my age
-19 years and counting, 4 assaults later, 0 years of
sobriety.

Exhausted

HAVE YOU EVER BEEN ASSAULTED?
HAVE YOU EVER BEEN JOLTED
IN THE MIDDLE OF THE NIGHT?
BECAUSE YOU WOKE UP WITH THE SAME OLD FRIGHT
THAT HE WAS VIOLATING YOU AGAIN

the middle of the afternoon?
morning?

what am I saying, the timing isn't important

Have you ever felt crushed?

have you ever put the blame on yourself, because you
didn't say no strong enough

Do they call you tough?
I understand why you don't feel like it

I don't feel like it either

it's like I'm weeping

I'm constantly seeping

blood everywhere

but he will never have to care

HE doesn't see my face when he looks over there

there is everywhere for me

and I'm sick of seeing
I close my eyes
and he's still right here

So when does he ever disappear?

On the occasion,
I think I was born with strength
other times I remember that
I was born with many dents
and I don't know if they can be repaired.
—universe help me out. this isn't fair.

I don't want to miss any of you

How can I miss an abuser?
How can I feel love so deeply?

for someone who hurt me continuously

it's hard to remember anything good
except for what I understood
at the time

to be love and friendship
I was blind
And that was all bullshit
for you at least.
but for me it was real

and I'd rather do anything but feel
the loss of you

—You were just there for so long now what do I do?

Dancing with Death

I'm dancing with death

I'm always out of breath

who knew I had so much depth

that I could perceive the threat

and still believe
my life was worth the bet

my advice to others is on the opposite side

it's never oh please go gamble with your life

it doesn't make things ok and it never makes them right

so stop doing what doesn't work

stop letting your mind be a jerk

to your own beautiful soul

stop dancing with death
let yourself grow old.

escapism

there are days when I cannot turn my wounding
into words

there are days when I want to leave the so called
world

there are days when typing on my phone won't
make the ache go away

there are days that people have to beg me to stay

And I wish I didn't worry everyone
who had to cross my path
but I'm in a cycle of constant relapse.
there are days for me that surviving isn't palatable

so I drink the whisky and I load the bowl
until I'm down another hole

fighting my life, fighting for my case

it's sad because every time
I get assaulted

I feel a part of me die

and a part of me tried
really hard to lie

I lied to myself every day for a while
for maybe three weeks
only then is when I began to weep
and grieve for the girl
who was violated too many times
in this cruel world.

You are a liar!!
I know they say it

So much crying

I feel I won't survive it
I don't even want to
But there is not an option
-who.
will fight for justice when I'm dead?

Traumatized beyond measure

I can't count the
amount of times
I've been assaulted.

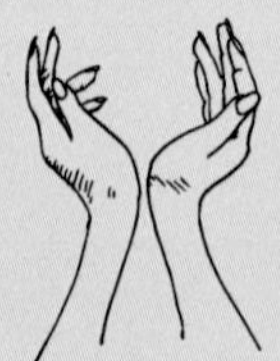

on one hand

or two

its way more than exhausting then they think

to be you.

Your I'm sorry's,

though you mean well
mean quite little to me

like thanks for the sympathy

but you didn't have to close the space between
your legs to get him to stop
or leave

tell me
when someone says stop

Is that a turn on?

-you are sick in the head but you think you've won.

No more excuses

abuse abuse
it's an excuse
you think it's that hard to not let loose?

abuse abuse
synced in rhythms with my rhymes

if I only had a dime
for every single time
someone has tried to extinct my shine
but I grabbed it back forcefully and took what was mine.

I have begged for hours that I would disappear
didn't you know that the devil lived here
not just physically
is what I meant
but he has a house
upstairs in my head

abuse abuse
in this shell of a human
abuse abuse
I didn't want to go through this

abuse abuse
you only forgot for a second
it never strays too far
you would think with the amount of bars
you might forget
but you don't

oh dearest
those memories are a curse
and I wouldn't wish them upon the worst of the worst
I know an apology didn't undo all that hurt.

I wanted to be whole
I wanted my soul
to breathe
—at least that was the goal
that I didn't achieve.

you survived the fire

let us not blame ourselves
For the ways we learned to endure the fire
When our lovers turn out liars
And our trust is broken beyond compare

We swear
We will never
give it away again
But then we do
10
Times over
And then finally
There comes a time
When a woman says
No.
No more
-the only goal I care to score

Lost in my trauma

I don't know how to do this thing

I don't know how to recover from so many painful stings

 I don't know how to erase the trauma

while he lives his life free of drama

my world was destroyed
by a stupid perverted boy

and now what the fuck do I do
with the memory of his sick voice

my heart shatters like a glass toy
trying to drown out the noise
and when he violated me so many times

why am I the one left with the guilt, when it all should have been his,

and not mine

aftermath

I'm in a field
of roses
Petals dripping
Down
thorns all around
throbbing through my shirt
I'll never put my body first
I don't care
what damage is done
as long as it's all in good fun
I'll make exceptions for thorns
but when I am reborn
into another lifetime
what will become of these horrors?

Once upon a time I loved my abuser

I can't stop thinking about you

and I wish I had left because of the sexual abuse
but I only left because my friends were begging me to..

I remember being at college and missing your soul

Please remind me
When did I get so old?

I miss you

but you are so incredibly dangerous

and the hate for what you did to my body, outweighs the
love enough for me to stay gone.

it doesn't matter anyways I was always a pawn

yet still

when I moved to California all I wanted was to hear your voice one last time

Even if it's toxic, your name will probably always make my eyes shine.

—I'll probably make the mistake of falling for you in every lifetime, I just hope in the next life I land on softer ground.

I am a woman

I embody grace
I embody rage
I do not need to host a
smile on my face

Why should I edit out the bad parts?
as though I have a pure angelic
heart

like trust me I am kind
until you decide that
I don't have a voice in my own
fucking rights

you want the word subservient
baked into a cake
a cake that you will make sure I bake
but what if instead I baked it with poison ivy
and you felt the that sting all over inside body
but you can't get medical help because
you'd be killing the plant cells
and uhh all lives matter

you want me in the kitchen
you want me to birth your children, too
but the truth
is that I'm not giving up
and your misogyny
will only get you as far as calling me a slut
as for my worth
I am more than just a vessel for BIRTH

pro life is a lie &
you don't care if people die
is what we chanted at the capitol
as 100s maybe a thousands or so
screamed
shouted
and I felt the pain in all our voices
such a moment of solidarity yet pure despair
like the world was falling apart but at least we had each
other there

but some will never hear us
and they'll sit on their knees
begging to a god that
no one can see

and one in which, might I add

they don't even believe in.

—But please go on about MY sins.

I can't help you if you won't even listen.

death calls more than life does

so like what do I do when I'm running on empty?

and death sits here always trying to tempt me

there used to be just whispers of pessimism
then I grew up a little
and while everyone told me
that my noise gets quieter as you get older
they were all liars
because that "noise"
only morphed into a frequency you could never understand

like just "have hope"

I'd rather choke

you have no idea
that I cannot stay afloat
I'm so fucking tired
And no one understands what I mean
so let me just break it down as simply
As I can

I am on a rollercoaster every single second of every single
day of every single year
and the tears
are always running off my face
and sometimes times I can't make myself eat so I just pace
I could go on to explain
the way I break off parts of me
for others happiness

but will never give myself the same love
the way that when people get mad it is as if a sword has
cut me and drawn blood
the marks on my arm that I wish would just disappear
the dissociation that doesn't allow me to sit in the here
and now
then there's substances which
seem good
until you
D
R
O
W
N.

PTSD

I'm drained
And I'm chained

and wanting to run
from myself, from the world

the sun
hasn't come out
for a trillion years.
I know you may see it
and tell me

you don't believe it
when I say

it's been storming every day
since I was fifteen

life is literally like a dream

but nothing like the fun ones where it's rainbows and ice cream

dissociation quite literally runs in my genes
no seriously I did a genetic test and turns out
I have won something in my life
a personality disorder

with an extra gift of a heavy heavy stigma

in this time
even having borderline
can seem like a crime.

and I'm always trying to escape to a world where things are fine.

but everything is chaos
& has always been chaos
I don't remember the date anymore and
sometimes not even the month
and my best friend came over a few weeks ago
and it was may and I thought it was November
because that is how much my trauma did a number
on me
—you can save yourself from the fire maybe but you can't
escape the ptsd.

roe v wade overturned survivors pov

my stupid world appears to have literally
just combusted in stupid flames
I'm so fucking angry and this feminine rage
has been truly awakened by your idiotic maze
of classist obstacles
so you call me a slut
a whore
but babe you forgot
how prepared us sluts are
to fight this war
-we dissent

<u>Longing for love</u>

I want to run into someone's arms
But there's only mine so I guess it will have to be
enough to keep me warm

today

but I don't want to be by myself
But I know that it will eventually help

I want to be with someone
I want comfort
someone who loves me with my shirt
on
and someone who's heart hurts
when I've been crying since dawn
he supports me when I'm in pain
he doesn't question me angerly asking where were you
again?
and
and I want a love that makes me feel free
but I also want someone to come home to and just drink
tea with
and I want to be independent
but I want to be in love
so fully
and joyfully
so marvelous together
but beautiful standing alone as well.
-they'll call us the sun and the moon, and our love will be
the strongest spell

So lost here

I stare at the search bar
I scroll through the internet searching for
whatever comes up when you search

I don't want to live anymore

or how do I kill myself fastest

and I look through every resource

which only enforces
the idea that I don't want to be here

I scroll until I run out of websites about suicide
prevention

and all that's left is song lyrics of pain

-fuck you life; you should be ashamed.

I hope I get her back

today all I did was cry
and I honestly barely pulled myself through
the fires

I stayed inside
nearly every minute
every hour
but my sadness doesn't spare
it devours

and I don't want to breathe
but I'm here and I can see
that people need
me to stay

but pushing through when every day

seems to be getting even longer
and more unbearable

is similar to walking through the scorching flames of hell

today self care looked like vertical lines of red marker on my legs
in hopes that I wouldn't self harm in the same place again
it worked
for today
I'm alive
for today
and that's truly the only positive thing I can say

but I hope that in a different reality
she doesn't even think about picking up that fucking razor

-because that girl used to be happy. I know because I
raised her.

You wouldn't get it

and when and if you ever get raped
Only then you will know
what's it like to crumble into your own grave
And be a slave
to your trauma
Only then you would understand
Only then would you know
why every survivor's heart broke
why we defend roe.

THE GUIDE: TO HEALING

Reporting an assault

You do not have to report your assault if you do not want to;

I have been in several situations where I felt extremely unsafe reporting because of possible severe backlash from perpetrators

—so this section only applies if you feel safe enough to do so.
Your story is just as valid whether it is reported or not.

Avenues:

Title IX process

Since I have been through this, I felt like I should shed some light on the issue.

If you are assaulted by a student on campus, this is the process you will go through.

If you want to pursue a trial you can, but my best advice would be to not expect the title IX administration to care just because the school/institution says they do.

When I went through my lengthy title IX case, I had proof of physical assaults from campus police, one other victim of rape, and one witness who saw me right after the assault shaken up and crying. Additionally, the perpetrator did admit to breaking consent on one occasion, but since we were in some form of relationship, consent was assumed somehow in the eyes of the panelists at the University of Redlands.

Police report (if outside of school/college) process

I have only reported to the police once, and this attempt was truly useless and did nothing but retraumatize me, all to tell me they could do literally nothing.

The woman officer told me that "you can't expect to say yes to one sexual act and not the other." implying it was my fault that he didn't understand even though I had made it so insanely clear.

You can shoot your shot and see if you can press charges. In my case, since I stopped his penis from entering me with my hand, it apparently did not mean anything to them.

So, if it was an assault where you were not penetrated or stopped it, they do not give a singular fuck. If you don't have evidence they will likely not take you seriously.

I encourage reporting if you can, but the results may not be in your favor in a country that thrives off the patriarchy, and it's important to keep this in mind.

To report to law enforcement– 

-go to the police station of the city it happened in and ask to report a sexual assault/rape

-You will be interviewed and asked to repeat your story several times so you need to mentally prepare.

-You will need to write down every detail on a piece of paper for them in pen and sign your name.

-They will contact you with further details.

Other avenues:

If you feel that your school or government has not done their job of issuing justice you can—

Take it to the government: you can report to the department of education; email them a copy of the complaint at OCR@ed.gov & the consent form found on this qr code

Equal Rights Advocacy Group can give you free legal advice; at the moment of writing this, they are at capacity, but they can give you referrals to other groups who might be able to help you.

advice@equalrights.org

Tips for healing from abuse and assault

When healing from rape/sexual assault, or multiple assaults, the process is going to be slow and it is going to be frustrating.

Healing is not linear, even though our brains can lie to us and tell us it is, and we are just somehow doing it wrong.

In fact healing is quite the opposite.

It is falling apart on the bathroom floor because you haven't let yourself be in your body for days.

It is messing up.

It is happy days.

But not all of a sudden.

Happiness comes in pockets for now, but we have hope that one day there will be an ocean overflowing with it. Healing is the days filled with mood swings and the days when you feel on top of the world even if it is just for a bit. It is those days when you can barely move and you just want the world to end but you stay, despite it all.

I'm going to share some of my coping skills and ways I am learning to heal myself, and I hope they help you on your journey. The pain is not going to go away ever. It isn't going to disappear one day. But it will get to a point where it won't occupy all your time and energy if you consciously work towards healing your trauma.

Mindful Journaling

A really good skill I learned in DBT is to observe your feelings rather than judge them. For example, when I have a really bad episode, I would write something like the following:

I AM NOTICING THAT I AM HAVING THE THOUGHT THAT I WANT TO DIE RIGHT NOW.

Next I ask myself okay well why is that? Approach your mind with curiosity instead of judgment. When pondering this, I can make a bullet pointed list of things triggering me or just word vomit what I feel is going wrong. This is a great tool for processing any event or trigger, whether heavy or not, especially if you don't feel like talking to someone else at that moment.

Structure to your day/planning/routines

Doing nothing all day is bound to make you sink deeper into your depression hole. Instead, give yourself some structure so your mind doesn't have all the time in the world to ruminate on the past. Below I will list some ideas for how to incorporate routine into your lifestyle.

MY TIPS FOR YOUR DAYS:)

- Start off your morning with gratitude

- Repeat positive affirmations to yourself, or play a video of someone else speaking them on loop while you shower or do another task, like brush your teeth

- Add some spirituality to your day—if you are spiritual, prayer might be calming for you, as well as other rituals that your particular religion/belief system resonates with.

- Start a course on something you are passionate about.

- Try to journal once a day—for me this is incredibly helpful for my dissociation as the ptsd has shook my sense of time. Writing down the date every day can be very beneficial when you can't recognize time is passing.

- Go to a coffee-shop! Some people prefer to work from home, but personally coffee shops really help my motivation and it is a nice way to interact with people without actually having to do a lot of talking. When you are extremely lonely, coffee shops or bookstores can be very comforting because there is no pressure to talk, but you also aren't alone and isolated.

Knowing your triggers

Self awareness is so insanely important during this process, and that means identifying what can trigger your flashbacks or episodes.

Everyone's triggers are different, but you can usually tell after dissecting your thought process a little bit.

For example, if you get a flashback, maybe try to see if there was a reason it came up.

If you are perhaps triggered into a depressive episode, look at the environmental factors that could have caused this like if you took your medication today (if you take meds) if you have been eating enough, and nourishing your body.

It is also important to note that oftentimes the people around us can trigger us, whether intentionally or not. Identifying and communicating your triggers with your loved ones will help your relationship.

Examples of triggers you may not realize:

—A drink you had with that person

—The smell of cologne/perfume

—Outfits you wore during traumatic time period

—Songs you heard during the trauma or after

—Times of year (your body carries the trauma and the same time of year of the incident can induce episodes)

—Trauma anniversaries: plan something on these days, and try to spend time with someone supportive

Tips for dealing with triggers and flashbacks

—breath control is key, use a breathing app if you find it hard to make yourself do.

This is so simple, yet so many people forget.

When you are going through a flashback, your breathing might get shallow.

The goal of mindful and deep breathing is to increase oxygen flow to your brain, so you can think a little more clearly.

—in emdr I was taught this breathing exercise called four tens; just breathe in, and hold your breath for 10 seconds, and release (repeat x4) this actually deprives your brain of oxygen during those 10 second intervals but as oxygen levels are restored as you finish the exercise,

this acts as a small reset for your brain when dealing with extremely hard triggers or intense emotions.

—give yourself a hug, put a hand on your shoulder and one around your waist; while your brain may know no other person is hugging you, your nervous system and body do not, and this can help you feel comforted if you are by yourself.

—buy stress balls, fidget toys, or other toys for stress relief

—at night it can be comforting to sleep with a large stuffed animal that you can hug (directly after coming home from my assault, this was insanely helpful)
—self validation/positive self talk

ex: I am safe right now. At this moment, no one is going to hurt me.

If you don't feel inclined to hook up with people or be sexually active, that is totally okay.

---------------------.

When one suffers a sexual assault or multiple, depending on how your individual brain processes it, you may become either hyposexual or hypersexual;

I have dealt with both, as I have been assaulted by three other men, but my recent assault has definitely made me more hyposexual.

Hyper and hyposexual after SA, essentially means that your sexual energy may increase severely, or you may do the exact opposite where you do not want to touch anyone most of the time, recognize that this is a normal after effect and is not something to be ashamed of.

However, I will say, that through my experience, mindless hookups have never been fulfilling to me, and if you are using sex as a means to self harm like I did at one point, you should definitely talk about that in therapy and try to both work through it and find other ways to support yourself so that you can keep yourself safe in future situations.

How to deal with victim blamers who cross your path

–shut down their statements validity immediately if you have energy/capacity

–remind yourself that if they were in your shoes, they would never say that; sometimes victim blamers are just uneducated; sometimes they are just stuck in a patriarchal mindset.
Feel free to educate them if you want, but if they don't listen, draw your boundaries.

–remind yourself that it wasn't your fault, no matter how many people try to convince you it was. No one would ask for that burden to carry.
Let all the blame fall on the perpetrator.

–if someone says, why were you drinking, or doing drugs, ect. remind yourself this is not a valid excuse for the perpetrators actions. It is very possible to be intoxicated and not assault people.

Also, the argument that if someone doesn't want to get raped they should just 'not drink' is silly. We deserved respect no matter what our intoxication level was during the time of assault.

a side note –remember, you don't owe people shit! if you don't want to even engage with ignorance and negativity, don't.

Therapy & Therapies

Therapy

Personally I think that everyone should be in therapy if it is financially possible.

Because therapy has so many benefits and in my opinion everyone should take time to work on themselves because no one is perfect and carefree.

I have Borderline Personality Disorder and Bipolar II so as you can imagine I have been through many years of therapy and it is probably the best way to work on yourself that exists.

But, you must keep in mind that just like every other field, there are bound to be therapists who just aren't good at their jobs.

Also sometimes you just don't vibe with a therapist, or two, that is okay—don't give up your search because the right therapist will be life changing.

I will go over some different forms of therapies that may potentially be helpful, but please research for yourself before going through with anything because you know your body better than anyone.

Cognitive Behavioral Therapy (CBT)

This is what you may think of as "regular" therapy, the most common form. CBT is very helpful and can be easily done at the same time as other therapies.

It is essentially talk therapy where you delve into your issues and attempt to address logical fallacies in your thought process.

It is always nice to hear a nonjudgmental viewpoint.

If you can't solve the problem by yourself, you likely need to see it from a different perspective.

Dialectical Behavioral Therapy (DBT)

DBT was originally made for those suffering with Borderline Personality Disorder(BPD) but it was later realized that it is helpful for every mental illness.

I have been in several DBT groups since fifteen and they have truly been so helpful because you get all these great tools and skills to help you cope with hard life events and triggers.

DBT doesn't have to be in a group setting though, and I have been in individual DBT as well.

I think both are very wonderful, but the groups are extremely validating because you get to see that you truly are not alone.

Eye movement desensitization and reprocessing (EMDR)

I am currently doing EMDR and it has been helping so far. EMDR is specialized PTSD/CPTSD or intense trauma therapy.

Any trauma is valid and worth working on if it occupies your mind all the time, but I am specifically hoping to heal my trauma from multiple sexual assaults.

EMDR is a heavy process, and insanely draining before it starts to get better so I would not recommend this until you are sure you are ready to face it all.

Listen to your own body and go at your own healing pace.
Below is an idea of how this therapy goes-

History intake

If you have CPTSD you likely have many traumatic events that you may need to work through.

The therapist will likely ask you to rank the different traumas and then start working with the least traumatic ones.

Coping/nervous system regulation resources

Your therapist should give you some tools to use both during emdr and outside;

examples could be breathing techniques, visualizations that calm the nervous system.

The main tool you will use during sessions is called bilateral stimulation.

Though this can be done with eye movement, it is a misconception that this is the only option.

For example as a survivor I do not feel super comfortable having someone that close to me when reliving those events, I use hand buzzers instead.

I hold them and it vibrates back and forth, you can also use audio bilateral stimulation where you would wear headphones and hear a beep alternating ears every time, or hand tapping back and forth by the therapist.

working through the traumatic event

1. You think about a vivid image of the incident

2. You link it to what that negative belief caused you to feel about yourself.
   Ex. "I cannot keep myself safe" or "it was my fault"

3. You sit in that belief for a bit.

4. Throughout the session you slowly morph it into a positive statement with the therapist helping you process everything that comes up

Biofeedback

Biofeedback is a type of therapy in which you can learn to control and improve your body's response to stimuli;

I haven't done this yet, but I plan to soon as it can help with a variety of mental health issues like anxiety, ADHD, PTSD/CPTSD, and many physical ailments as well, like asthma and IBS.

During biofeedback you will learn to regulate your body with a variety of different tools and by measuring brain waves, breathing, heart rate, muscle contractions, sweat gland activity, and temperature.

This is a really great option because it is quite successful and non invasive.

Esketamine

Esketamine is FDA approved to treat MDD (MAJOR DEPRESSIVE DISORDER) either nasally or through an IV.

I have done this therapy; I only saw some improvement in the first two weeks, even though I did it twice a week for several weeks.

However, it is important to understand that everyone's brain reacts differently to different medications and something that did not work for me may work for someone else.

I am also diagnosed with BPD and Bipolar 2 co-occurring, so the depression diagnosis is really only part of the puzzle.

ACTIVISM TIPS

—stay aware of your surroundings at all times—if you see a suspicious character at a protest, and they aren't armed, simply move to a different part of the crowd.

—if someone is armed who is clearly not the group you are supporting, run—this is why you MUST stay aware

—keep in mind the police can arrest you for peacefully protesting at times—write a number in permanent marker to bail you out—for example, a nonprofit with lawyers who assist protestors with bail.

—turn your face ID off, keep your phone locked with a password in case of arrest

—when speaking about important matters use an app that is end to end encrypted like Signal

—delete your period tracking apps, your data can be sold easily

How to protest without rallying on the streets:

—write articles about topics important to you; Medium is an easy platform to use that is free

—share your thoughts on social media, instagram, twitter, facebook, tik tok

—sing about your frustration at a coffee shop or open mic or write poetry like me!

-call your representatives; email them; and send mail to them; the louder the better-wear them down. (all their info can be found online)

—donate to pro abortion funds

—donate to pro abortion and pro choice campaigns
—sit ins in government buildings ex. The Capitol

—volunteer and help out individually with a campaign

—Be loud in your opinions, and don't pay attention to those who say you are too invested—these are OUR RIGHTS—of course we are invested.

—Speak at a town hall meeting and voice your concerns to your county's representative. I have done this twice and though I can't necessarily change someone's mind overnight, I can plant seeds of doubt in the audience's mind and point out flaws in logic publicly.

THANK YOU FOR READING!

You can find my other books and articles on my link tree!

WRITTEN BY TARA KAUR SACHAR

author, poet, activist, survivor, human rights advocate

Designed by Namisha Kaur
CONTACT FOR DESIGN/FULL-STACK DEVELOPMENT:
namishakaur0@gmail.com

Made in the USA
Columbia, SC
04 April 2023